AF372623

Copyright

1. Copyright Notice
Copyright © [2023] [Chumki]

2. Rights and Permissions:

3. Edition and Country of Printing
1st edition- India

2nd edition-India and Internationally.

4. Publisher Information

Year of 1st publication- 2023
Year of 2nd edition- 2023

Initially it(1st edition) was published in India through Notion Press. Later it (the 2nd edition) is published as an e-Book in various international platforms through draft2digital.

Other details of the Book published in Notion press.
1. Product Id- 337709-1393764-NA-NED-TO-NIKI-REG-IND-DIY-070623-0
2. Format –Paper Back
3. Book Size-6/9
4. Pages-(1st edition)-42 pages, 2nd edition (72 pages)

<u>TITLE PAGE</u>

NAME OF THE BOOK- THE
PURPOSE OF HUMAN BIRTH

AUTHOR- CHUMKI

1ST PUBLICATION- IN INDIA,
NOTION PRESS/ YEAR 2023

2ND PUBLICATION TRHOUGH-
INTERNATIONALLY BY
DRAFT2DIGITAL

Chapter 1- Time is limited and precious; So don't waste time in context of spiritual realisation.

As days passes, you loose time from your life span. Little does people realises that we have come here on this earth for a limited time. So when we think of loosing time means we are destroying a major portion of our lifetime in purposes not designed by God for sending us here. The time factor is very very essential from spiritual point of view.

When I speak of don't waste time, I mean that time is valuable from spiritual point of view. If we destroy time, time will destroy us. The spirit is all that matters. We have been given a human birth after suffering from many many different species of birth whereby we have become plants, animals, insects, flying insects, water animals etc. that was the time when we did not have the capacity to think and understand because it was not given to us by God. We are given this capacity only in this human form of birth.

As we age, our power to comprehend things, practices sadhana and doing meditative practices gradually declines. So we should undertake the spiritual practices from birth itself. Because except practising devotional service to lord, we don't have actually any other duty in this impermanent materialistic life for which we are wasting our valuable time and energy. From the sloka below, you can understand, that truly nothing is permanent and everything is transitory in this world of continuous birth and death.

जीवितं क्षणविनाशिशाश्वतं किमपि नात्र।

अर्थ: यह क्षणभुंगर जीवन में कुछ भी शाश्वत नहीं है।

In every scriptures, it is declared that human birth is impermanent and can be snatched away by the Lord of death, Yama without prior notice. So it is of utmost importance we take this life seriously for self-realisation and attain the Lord eternal abode before we leave this material world. It is then we can be freed from repeated birth and death.

We get the human birth after moving through many species of life for many kalpas. One kalpa is one day of Brahma and equals one night of Brahma.

सहस्रयुगपर्यन्तमहर्यद्ब्रह्मणो विदुः ।
रात्रिं युगसहस्रान्तां तेऽहोरात्रविदो जनाः ॥ 17॥

sahasra-yuga-paryantam ahar yad brahmano viduh
rātrim yuga-sahasrāntām te 'ho-rātra-vido janāh

▶ 0:00 / 0:21   🔊 ⋮

sahasra— one thousand ; *yuga*— age ; *paryantam*— until ; *ahah*— one day ; *yat*— which ; *brahmanah*— of Brahma ; *viduh*— know ; *rātrim*— night ; *yuga-sahasra-antām*— lasts one thousand yugas ; *te*— they : *ahah-rātra-vidah*— those who know this day and night ; *janāh*— people

sahasra-yuga-paryantam ahar yad brahmano viduh
rātrim yuga-sahasrantam te 'ho-rātra-vido janah

Translation

BG 8.17: One day of Brahma (*kalp*) lasts a thousand cycles of the four ages (*mahā yug*) and his night also extends for the same span of time. The wise who know this understand the reality about day and night.

Chapter 2- We have no power to attain God by our own spiritual practices

In last chapter, I talked of age and spiritual practices correlation. But spiritual practices can only help to know the truth, to purify ourselves. By no means our spiritual practices can help us attain God. It can only make ready the plate(patra) for receiving the divine love of the Lord. It is the lord himself who help us to attain him. It is his decision to grant us his divine love and abode. We are helpless by ourselves even to raise a cup of tea without divine grace and desire. The Lord is always eager to grace us with his kripa or blessings to grant us liberation, all he wants is our turning away from world and materialistic desires and turn towards him with all our heart and love. *It is like when a mother finds the child is happy with toys, she lets the child plays with it, but when the child is bored out of playing with toys, the mother eagerly goes and takes hold of and nurture the child with love and care.*

So here, I would like to point out that we have a great responsibility on our own shoulder to get our share of liberation from the cycle of repeated births and deaths for which exactly the purpose of human birth is described in the scriptures of Santana dharma.

A quote of Sri Sankaracharya from Bhaja Govindam, clearly defines why are we born as human beings in this earth.

भज गोविन्दम्

Bhaja Govindam

द्वादशमञ्जरिका

1. Dvadasamanjarika

भज गोविन्दं भज गोविन्दं
भज गोविन्दं मूढमते ।
संप्राप्ते सन्निहिते काले
नहि नहि रक्षति 'डुकृञ् करणे' ॥

Bhaja govindam bhaja govindam
Bhaja govindam mudhamate
Samprapte sannihite kale
Nahi nahi raksati dukrana karane.

Worship Govinda, worship Govinda,
Worship Govinda, foolish one!
Rules of grammar profit nothing
Once the hour of death draws nigh.

Here Govinda means, Lord Krishna or the divine personality. We are born to praise the lord, or in simple words we have in reality one duty i.e love the divine. For loving the divine lord Krishna, is the purpose of human birth is the statement with utmost simplicity for the general mass.

The above verse from Bhaja Govindam says that if we do not worship the lord within the prescribed time limit, then when the time will end of this human birth, our knowledge (here it says rules of grammar; which signifies worldly knowledge, achievements, relations etc.) will not be able to save us again from falling to the pangs of repeated birth and death i.e Maya or illusion. If we do not take proper steps to come out of this vicious circle of birth and death by realising the purpose of human birth, then again by laws made by the Lord, we will be send to the illusory world to suffer in 84 lakh species.

In this world everything can be achieved by our own efforts because everything we intend or desire to achieve is material and the effort we put also is material. So the things of the world within human capacity can be achieved by material efforts and knowledge. *But the divine can be achieved by the divine grace only.* How can the sadhana or the spiritual practices that we practice which are material in nature make us attain the divine lord. But yes the sadhana or the spiritual practices can just help us to make our sanskaras (of past life impressions) pure and it will make us eligible to attain the divine love of the Lord which will be awarded to us by the divine lord only. The sadhanas or spiritual practices only help us to go beyond the three modes of material nature, rajas, tamas and satvas and be situated in the true self i.e the soul.

पुनरपि जननं पुनरपि मरणं
पुनरपि जननीजठरे शयनम् ।
इह संसारे बहुदुस्तारे
कृपयाऽपारे पाहि मुरारे ॥ २१ ॥

Born again, death again, again to stay in the mother's womb !
It is indeed hard to cross this boundless ocean of samsAra. Oh
Murari ! Redeem me through Thy mercy.

Stanza attributed to nityanAtha.

Another sloka of Bhaja Govindam, speaks that we are born innumerable times and are dead innumerable times. It is difficult to free ourselves and cross the boundless ocean of samsaras. So the soul bound by maya calls to the lord that you liberate me by your mercy or kripa i.e you can use your divine grace to free me out of the vicious circle of birth and death, and I by no means by my own sadhana can cross the ocean of illusion or maya. So in this verse it is clear, that no one in this world of maya has power to free oneself; only by the divine grace of the Lord can one free oneself. The divine grace is achieved simply by loving the Lord unconditionally and surrendering to the Lord hundred percent without thinking oneself to be the doer of all that we are doing with the Lord's power. In simple terms we are only one instrument in the hands of the God.

Chapter3- Realise the importance of human birth

As said earlier human birth is precious as in this birth only we can attain the divine realm and free ourselves from the cycle of repeated birth and death and wandering in 84 lakh species. When we once reach the divine realm, we never have to come back to this material world. As is clear from the sloka below from Bhagwad gita (15.6)

na tad bhāsayate sūryo
na śaśāṅko na pāvakaḥ
yad gatvā na nivartante
tad dhāma paramaṁ mama

The nature of this material world is darkness, but the spiritual world is full of light and yet is not illumined by fire or electricity. Kṛṣṇa hints of this in the fifteenth chapter of the Bhagavad-gītā (15.6).

"That abode of Mine is not illumined by the sun or moon, nor by electricity. One who reaches it never returns to this material world."

In other forms of birth, the power to attain the divine does not exist. As in lower species of human birth as fish, animals, birds, they are born only to enjoy, eat, sleep, have sex, procure progeny and die. But in human birth there is the power to contemplate, comprehend and realise the divine and accumulate knowledge through a self-realised teacher who has gained experience in spiritual path. Here in this human birth we should question "who is I?", "Why have I come to this earth?", "Where will I go after death?" etc. In Human form of birth we can analyse things, search for knowledge and practice what is needed to achieve the ultimate goal of life i.e God.

Even learning the scripture of Bhagwad Gita can help one attain perfect insight into purpose of human birth, what is our duty, and how to attain the Lord. In Hinduism the divine, the ultimate reality is God and his names are innumerable but one main name is Krishna. Most of the saints call him Krishna, Rama, Hari, Vasudeva.

About the power of Bhagwad Gita the great saint Adi Sankaracharya has written in his poem Bhaja Govindam as follows-

भगवद्गीता किञ्चिदधीता
गङ्गाजललवकणिका पीता ।
सकृदपि येन मुरारिसमर्चा
क्रियते तस्य यमेन न चर्चा ॥ २० ॥

bhagavad gītā kiñcidadhītā
gaṇgā jalalava kaṇikāpītā |
sakṛdapi yena murāri samarcā
kriyate tasya yamena na carcā || 20

The translation for the above sloka of Bhagwad Gita is-

"For him, who has studied the Bhagavad gitá even a little, who has drunk a drop of the Gañgá-water, and who has performed the worship of the Destroyer of the demon Mura at least once, i.e Lord Govinda (Krishna) there is no tiff with Yama (the lord of death)."

Narada Pancaratra states:

sarvopādhi-vinirmuktaṁ
tat-paratvena nirmalam
hṛṣīkeṇa hṛṣīkeśa-sevanaṁ
bhaktir ucyate

Translation: "When one is freed from the false designations (in relation with the body) of this world, one is purified (and thus becomes qualified to obtain real knowledge)."

The temporary designations of human beings as doctors, engineers, scientists etc. are only with relation to body. Once the soul leaves the body, the body is a dead element and the designations are meaningless. So to realise the importance of human birth is to realise the temporary nature of body, mind and ego. So no need to run after sense pleasures which we get to enjoy in other forms of birth as insects, animals, birds, demi gods etc. So the human birth is to achieve knowledge of the supreme and get ourselves freed from the shackles of illusion or maya.

The human form being rare we need to quickly realise its importance and act accordingly. The human form of birth is important because it has the power to unite us with our eternal companion, Sri Sri Radha Krishna and return to our home and free ourselves from this worldly life of repeated births and deaths, pleasures and pain, heat and cold, praise and humiliation, health and diseases, union and separation etc. In short, in human life we have the power to go beyond death, to achieve eternal peace and unending happiness. It is said in scriptures that the nature of material happiness is such that it is temporary and is ever declining. The more we enjoy materialistic pleasures, it soon becomes less and less.

Actually one term in economics subject is diminishing marginal utility, which says the more and more as we enjoy a particular object the less and less enjoyable it becomes and after a point of time, we would not like to have one more additional bit of it. Similarly, the materialistic pleasures are such that the more and more we enjoy an object, or people, or food or whatever, it gradually comes to a point of boredom or no more having the power to catch our interests as earlier. Not only that it also turns into the opposite form of pleasure giving i.e it starts making us sad or angry after a certain point of time.

Chapter 4- Start the journey of attaining the Lord through small steps and easy practices.

In this book titled the purpose of human birth, the author desires to make the readers aware of the reason a human is born as a human. It is only after that, who is a total neophyte to this knowledge will achieve some insight related to the purpose of our birth as human beings. *Until and unless a person gains the knowledge on the purpose of human birth, he continues to assumes that we as animals have come here to eat, sleep, mate, have babies, make a house, accumulate wealth and security and then die helplessly*. He do not realise that there is a greater reason for our birth as human beings and if we do not know or pay heed to it, we will suffer for infinite time(kalpas) with innumerable pain which is beyond our comprehending capability.

So in simple language, the author has tried to explain that we need to first understand the reason of our birth, and then how to achieve the goal for which we are gifted or awarded this human form. A layman who has no knowledge of the Vedic scriptures will be confused and worried if at once you just force him or her to do things which he has no capacity to do or understand. So step by step a neophyte has to go through the correct knowledge and then realise his duty to realise the goal of life and act accordingly if convinced.

As human beings are covered by Maya or illusion, they cannot at once and easily digest the spiritual knowledge. They have to go slowly, understanding tiny spiritual facts and then take small steps. Another reason is, there are four yugas in a time span and now we are going through kali yuga or the age of hypocrisy. In this age of kali, different spiritual practices as japa, tapa, yagna are no longer possible due to the impurities of present times and small life span and less mental abilities of people compared to satya yuga, dwapara and treata yuga. So we can take the small initial steps to attain knowledge and then divine love or prema for the lord or Krishna in simple words.

The first step a lay man can do is first gain basic knowledge of Hindu scriptures. For this rather than reading this and that book of different authors, one can start from Bhagwad Gita. Why read Bhagwad Gita, because Vedas are huge and vast and it is not possible in today's fast moving and complex times, to gain access to all the Vedas as most of them are lost in passing time, secondly it is not easy to understand them in today's context without a bonafide Guru or teacher who has all knowledge. But as Srimad Bhagwad Gita and Srimad Bhagawadam are the two scriptures which are the essence of the entire Vedic scriptures.

Even among the two scriptures, for a neophyte in spiritual path, the Bhagwad Gita is the most practical teacher in form of book and is told by the Lord himself to his friend cum devotee, Arjuna. Srimad Bhagawadam will be digestible(graspable) only once you realise who is Lord, Brahman, or Krishna, then how to attain him, ie through love, karma yoga and gyana yoga; the easiest way being love towards Brahman i.e, Bhakti Yoga and how to get that love, by knowing the leelas or pass-times of the Lord, the qualities of the Lord, power, beauty, and effulgence of the Lord and these elaborate descriptions are there in Srimad Bhagawadam.

So first step towards self-realisation in this age of quarrel and hypocrisy (Kali) is read the Sri Bhagwad Gita, which will first explain the practical way of living life, dealing with problems, getting over anxiety, moving beyond pain and pleasures, working with equanimity of benefits and loss, dedicating the fruits of actions to the Lord and get established in Karma Yoga etc. So once we are practically able to see the material problems and solve them with ease, then we will be prepared for a mind-set to start knowing Brhaman, knowing ourselves, our relations with the Lord and then attain devotion and finally liberation through love to attain the Lord.

So in nutshell, for people inquisitive of spiritual liberation and attainment of liberation, the foremost step is to read the Bhagwad Gita, then after being little clear on concepts of Bhagwad Gita, go in-depth for Srimad Bhagawadam and then the process will automatically be enlightened by the Lord and he will himself guide you towards the Supreme.

The Bhagwad Gita is written in almost all languages and wherever one may be one i.e. in any country of any language can easily read and understand Bhagwad Gita. Once you are comfortable reading the Gita, then comes the next step, gradually try to understand the slokas of the Gita and relate it to practicality. Gradually and gradually you can understand, that every single human doubts are resolved in the Bhagwad Gita by the Almighty i.e Lord Krishna himself. What authentic source of knowledge can you have than from the mouth of the Lord himself.

Bhagwad Gita, chapter 2 verse 11

श्रीभगवानुवाच
अशोच्यानन्वशोचस्त्वं प्रज्ञावादांश्च भाषसे ।
गतासूनगतासूंश्च नानुशोचन्ति पण्डिताः ॥ ११ ॥

For eg. the above sloka of Bhagwad Gita, says that

Lord Kṛṣṇa said: you are mourning for those not worthy of sorrow; yet speaking like one knowledgeable. The learned neither laments for the dead or the living.

In the above slokas, the Lord Krishna says Arjuna is unnecessarily mourning for the upcoming events of the war to happen. As he explains that is not at all wise to lament for the dead or the living because the dead is bound to be born again and the alive is bound to die. So in both ways that which is bound to happen, and impossible to evade, what is the benefit for mourning for such an event.

Bhagwad Gita, chapter 2 verse 12

Any simple person can understand that Lord in the above sloka says, that time is for you and me but God is beyond time. The Lord says, there was not a time when the Lord did not exist nor we neither will a time come when neither the Lord nor we will cease to exist. That means there is something beyond this body that is always there and to whom the Lord addresses. If the Lord is addressing Arjuna in the above sloka he meant it for the soul of Arjuna and not the body of Arjuna as the body of Arjuna to whom the Lord was speaking is subjected to birth and death. So gradually the Slokas of Bhagwad Gita opens eyes i.e spiritual insights of a neophyte or a layman in the spiritual path to knowledge.

Then one can practice listening to the verses of Bhagwad Gita slokas with explanation from an experience sadguru. There are many rasik saints in Vrindavan and always were there, who having done penances in their previous births are so well versed in the knowledge of Hindu scriptures without even touching or reading the scriptures in this life. Such is the impact of self-realisation. It cleanses your soul. It breaks the bondages of innumerable past lives and make our soul self-realised by the divine grace.

When we practically go to a self-realised saint in tirtha sthana or places of pilgrimages that we gain a lot of blessings and knowledge by their grace which itself has the power to break the bondages from many many lives of ignorance. It is said your own sadhana cannot do in lives which can do to you by grace of a self-realised saint.

Besides, one may argue that in today's chaotic world it is not possible to visit the places of pilgrimages, and practically visit saints and listen to their discourses. No problem; the author totally relates to your circumstances. So there is one best opportunity that is available in today's worlds of busy lives i.e technology. *By use of your computers, mobiles and other electronic devices you can listen to the discourses of very renowned saints from the comfort of your homes and in your free time without having to visit places of spiritual importance or pilgrimages.*

You can listen to what they say and understand. Not only that you should very well try to bring into your practical life by following those practices that they ask us to do to attain divine grace.

For eg. a very famous spiritual Guru, Sri Hit Premanand Govind Sharan Ji Maharaj ji of these time (year

2023) staying in Vrindavan gives his discourses in plain simple understandable language relating to the simplest of paths to attain the divine prema. It is very easy to hear and watch though you-tube. *Daily his discourses of one to two hours are uploaded in YouTube and those valuables are so easy to obtain but the main thing is one needs to develop interests and patience to hear them daily, contemplate them and bring them into daily practices so that they can attain that goal easily* which would have been difficult to attain otherwise had the presence of technology would not been there.

 His teachings are too simple and beautiful. He supports his teachings by quoting relevant verses from the scriptures. The author means to say there is nothing the saint speaks of his mind, but what is in the scriptures supported by the rasik saints practical experiences about the divine prema and path.

As far as the author is concerned, she herself follows the Guru Maharaj ji, Sri Hit Premanand Govind sharan ji and gains a lot of strengths to face the difficulties of her day to day life which are never ending and very painful, by his divine grace. The author is writing this book to show the paths to layman, who are troubled in life and who want to attain the spiritual knowledge and go back to the eternal abode of Lord Hari from which one has not to return back. The author mentions that really she does not know the level of spiritual maturity she has but she is trying to be into this path but at least she prays others can benefit from small methods of teachings that she herself have found helpful and also learnt from various scriptures, books and saints.

Start the journey of realising God through small steps means that we should gradually practice step by step gaining knowledge of the ultimate, then reading about the Vedas and Hindu scriptures as Bhagwad Gita and Srimad Bhagawadam, then listening to discourses from the actually realised saints and by remembering and chanting the names of Lord Hari or say Krishna. So realising God is not a very difficult thing, it is actually done by small steps but it has to be done with sincerity, gradually and in a persistent manner. The other thing important in spiritualism is interests. A sincere devotee can continue his practices if his interests gradually shifts from worldly attractions to the divine path.

For eg. every scriptures stresses on the loving remembrance of the Lord all the time and this thing can be established only on practising the same every day and every hour. Gradually it will become a habit that we can't live without remembering our beloved Lord. As we all in human relationships desires security and love in any kind of dealing so is the Lord, who wants that we should love him in a way that we don't love the same to any other person or things or events of the world. i.e our minds should be exclusively attached to the lord (ananya bhakti) and not to the world at the same time. A sloka of Bhagawad Gita says how to remember the Lord to be able to attain him.

अनन्याश्चिन्तयन्तो मां ये जनाः पर्युपासते |
तेषां नित्याभियुक्तानां योगक्षेमं वहाम्यहम् || 22||

ananyāsh chintayanto māṁ ye janāḥ paryupāsate
teshāṁ nityābhiyuktānāṁ yoga-kshemaṁ vahāmyaham

BG 9.22: There are those who always think of Me and engage in exclusive devotion to Me. To them, whose minds are always absorbed in Me, I provide what they lack and preserve what they already possess.

In another sloka of Bhagwad Gita, Lord Krishna says

समोऽहं सर्वभूतेषु न मे द्वेष्योऽस्ति न प्रियः |
ये भजन्ति तु मां भक्त्या मयि ते तेषु चाप्यहम् || 29||

samo 'haṁ sarva-bhūteshu na me dveshyo 'sti na priyaḥ
ye bhajanti tu māṁ bhaktyā mayi te teshu chāpyaham

BG 9.29: I am equally disposed to all living beings; I am neither inimical nor partial to anyone. But the devotees who worship Me with love reside in Me and I reside in them.

Even the Lord says, that by constant remembrance of me the devotee can attain me without doubt. The same is said by the sloka of Bhagwad Gita.

मन्मना भव मद्भक्तो मद्याजी मां नमस्कुरु |
मामेवैष्यसि युक्त्वैवमात्मानं मत्परायणः || 34||

man-manā bhava mad-bhakto mad-yājī māṁ namaskuru
māṁ evaiṣhyasi yuktvaivam ātmānaṁ mat-parāyaṇaḥ

BG 9.34: **Always think of Me, be devoted to Me, worship Me, and offer obeisance to Me. Having dedicated your mind and body to Me, you will certainly come to Me.**

Chapter 5 - If you know nothing, then just remember the Lord every second with love giving up all others expectations from the world

The fruits of all scriptures is attain love towards the Lord. In simple words, the main goal of human birth, the teachings of all Hindu and other scriptures point out at one thing, i.e the path or methodology to attain diving love for the Lord or say divya prema.

So here the author explains her readers the main method to please God and attain his proximity is to constantly remember him. *What better method to remember God than to chant his divine names*. See, the Lord has no doubt innumerable names but the main names or one which catches your interests are the ones you should chant. Not only chant but at the same time, you need to contemplate on the form of the Lord which you love say Radharani, Or Krishna or Radha Krishna divine forms, or Nrisimha, or Rama etc. But the one which is the major forms and names as per Hindu scriptures is that of the Lord Krishna. So thinking of Lord Krishna we can constantly chant his names to attain the divine love and abode of Krishna. Second, the scriptures explains there is no difference between the names of Lord and the Lord himself. So when we chant the names of Lord Krishna, Lord Krishna himself dances in our tongue.

There are verses from scriptures which elaborates the importance of remembering and chanting lord's names. For example,

Sri Chaitanya-Charitamrita says –

"The name of Sri Ramchandra grants liberation – hence it is 'tarak' (the liberator), however the name of Sri Krishna gives prem, therefore it is 'parak' (the One Who gives love)." – (C.C.antya.3.244).

One sinful person named Ajamila who had done every type of sinful actions in his life, starting from falling for love with a prostitute, abandoning one's faithful wife, gambling, cheating his family and taking away all their wealth for satisfying his beloved prostitute friend, but still was delivered at the time of death because he was calling out of illusion or attachment to his smallest son whose name was Narayana. So unknowingly without any intention of his chanting the divine name, just because he was remembering his son named Narayana at the time of death, he was not taken by the yama duta and was relieved by Vishnu dutas(servants of Lord Vishnu) for all his sins and was allowed to evade death.

Deliverance of Ajamila on taking the name of Lord Narayana

So is the name of the Lord divine as the Lord himself and has every power to deliver a soul if he remembers particularly at time of death. No doubt remembering the Lord's name every moment equally helps a soul to remember the Lord at times of calamities or at times of death but even if a person is unable to remember the Lord's name during death time due to severe pain or unconscious state, still if he was taking the name throughout life then the Lord himself comes to the person in death bed to remember him and deliver him. Secondly the name of lord has the power to purify a person from the sins of innumerable births and take him beyond Maya or illusion.

As said by lord Chaitanya in Chaitanyamrita

ayam hi krta-nirveso janma-koty-amhasam api
yad vyajahara vivaso nama svasty-ayanam hareh
(Srimad Bhagavatm, 6.2.7)

(The Vishnu-Dutas said) Ajamila has already atoned for all his sinful actions. Indeed, he has atoned not only for sins performed in this life but also for those he had performed in millions of lives. It is because he had chanted the holy name of Narayana in a helpless condition.

Chapter 6- Realise the   pain of the soul in wandering in 84 lakh species

Very few people know that we are granted human birth by the infinite mercy of Lord Hari and it is something we will not achieve just like that and that to time and again. We have come to the human species only after crossing the 84 lakh species and that to innumerable times (for kalpas) and again if we do not serve the purpose for which human birth is given to us, again we will be sent to the same different lower forms of births.

So a human being is given at the maximum of 100 years to live. This again is not possible in today's time(i.e kali yuga) when everything is so chaotic, complex, food unnatural and agriculture uses a lot of chemical fertilisers and pesticides, there is so many types of new diseases which has made the longevity of human life very less. So in such times of age of hypocrisy or in layman's voice the Kali-yuga as per Hindu Sastras, we have one option to attain the path of God and that is the easiest is to know and love god, remember his name and chant his name. This method is also something recommended by the author out of   the Hindu scriptures.

The Bṛhan-Nāradīya Purāṇa recommends:

harer nāma harer nāma harer nāmaiva kevalam
kalau nāsty eva nāsty eva nāsty eva gatir anyathā

In this Age of Kali, *hari-kīrtana* is very, very important. The importance of chanting the holy name of the Lord is stated in the following verses from *Śrīmad-Bhāgavatam* (12.3.51-52):

kaler doṣa-nidhe rājann
asti hy eko mahān guṇaḥ
kīrtanād eva kṛṣṇasya
mukta-saṅgaḥ paraṁ vrajet

kṛte yad dhyāyato viṣṇuṁ
tretāyāṁ yajato makhaiḥ
dvāpare paricaryāyāṁ
kalau tad dhari-kīrtanāt

This is stated in Vishnu Purana like this:

jala-ja   nava-laksani   sthavara   laksa-vimsati
krmayo rudra-sankhyakah paksinam dasa-laksanam
trimsal-laksani pasavah catur-laksani manusah

"There are 900,000 species living in the water. There are also 2,000,000 non-moving living entities (sthavara), such as trees and plants. There are also 1,100,000 species of insects and reptiles, and there are 1,000,000 species of birds. As far as quadrupeds are concerned, there are 3,000,000 varieties, and there are **400,000 human species.**"

Total comes 84 LAKHS TYPES OF SPECIES/ BIRTHS.

The pain felt by the soul in 84 lakh species bodies is beyond our intellectual grasping capacity now while we are in human form. We are born sometimes as animals, as birds, as reptiles, as fish and animals living in water, sometimes as reptiles, sometimes as insects etc. accordingly we suffer the condition of that form of birth. As animals we become food for other animals, we have to bear the heat and cold just as in human birth, we don't have intellectual capability or mental thinking capacity. As animals we become food for other animals and however cleverly we try to hide or protect ourselves from our prey, we become helplessly their food. So we are in a way trapped in a phase from where we can be freed only by the mercy of the Lord and that mercy is an sympathetic awarding of human birth by the Lord and when the Lord blesses us with a human birth, his only condition to free us from the   repeated cycle of birth and death is by knowledge of the eternal truth, realising the purpose of human birth and service of the lord with love (prema) and constant loving remembrance of the lord.

Chapter 7- Take to the practice of hearing the spiritual discourses from a self-realised saint

How many scriptures we may read, but until and unless we hear the valuable teachings of a self -realised rasik saints, we cannot attain that divine love for God. The self-realised rasik saints are the one who have actually attained the divine love and felt that eternal happiness which is beyond the materialistic happiness which is always declining and as a fire, how much butter you add to the fire, it burns more and do not extinguish.

The rasik saints explains the Hindu scriptures in practical way so that normal man can easily understand and grasp them; not only that they can apply the same in their day to day life and practices.

For eg. the author has mentioned in her earlier paragraphs in this book, about the famous Vaishnava of present time in year 2023, the rasik saint of Vrindavan Sri Hit Premanand Guru Maharaj Ji. If you go through his teachings, in youtube, or his web contents, you can realise how valuable they are. *The Guru Maharaj Ji has explained the great teachings in very simple and practical manner. His disciplines are running mainly three important channels as Sri Hit Radha kripa, Bhajan Marg and Ekantik Vartalap.*

The author suggests her book readers should without delay go through these channels to gain insight into the jewel of knowledge of Hindu scriptures and attain the divine prema of the Lord which would not have been otherwise possible to get had the technology not been there for us.

Not only Guru Maharaj, there are other gurus quite knowledgeable of Hindu scriptures, you can go to their online portal and gain sufficient knowledge on the Hindu scriptures.

Another one was Kripalu ji Maharaj ji also who has already left his body for heavenly abode. You can go through his teachings in form of YouTube, books and discourses spread by his disciples. He also explains the impermanency of life, the uselessness of material pursuits and importance of attaining knowledge of the absolute truth and attain divine abode within limited time by constant remembrance and contemplation of the eternal form of Sri Sri Radha Krishna.

Chapter 8- There is no simpler way to attain God then to realise him as your own and surrender

Until we will be taking the responsibility of karmas on our own shoulder, we will have to handle the pain and pleasure, the repeated birth and death pangs, the sufferings of 84 lakh species etc.; in simple language we have to remain bonded or bound by Maya or illusion. So where is the case of freedom when we cannot free our shoulders from the burden of death and birth. So when we surrender to Krishna he takes the responsibility with himself. He burns the results of both our sinful and pious actions so that the results will not be in a position to be fruitful i.e. he burns the powers of seed to gets fruitful.

In the title of chapter 8, the author writes that there is no way to attain God then to make him his own. Try to understand the depth of the sentence. How can we make someone our own when that person is already our own. See in simple terms the author is explaining. We all know the relationships are flickering but what may come our parents are our dearest and our own. We don't have to remember, establish or force the facts upon anyone to prove that our parents are our own. Only we need to show our love and acknowledgment for the unconditional love they have been giving us. It is not that we are making them our own but we are reinforcing the love they have given to us back to them so that it shows the reciprocity of children's love for their parents.

Similarly, the love with God is beyond the material conception of love. It is eternal and divine and never changing. The material love with people, with relatives, with siblings, partner, lovers, even with parents is based on some sort of conditions or business but the love of god for all the souls in this world is unconditional and is not with any expectations form the lord's side.

The lord himself in various scriptures mentions the need of the souls to surrender to him and loving him to gain his eternal companionship and get freedom or liberation from material bondage. He does not demand anything from us and he only desires that we turn to him instead of turning towards the world. He wants us to love him only and not the world at the same time. i.e we should desire the lord alone and we can't desire the world at the same time is the only condition. It is as simple as this. A mother gives toys to her children to play. So long as the children are satisfied with the toys they don't need the companion of the mother. But when they get bored from playing with the toys and wants the mother to take hold of the child, the mother comes running to take care of the child. Similarly, is the condition of we souls. God has given us a temporary playground i.e this illusionary world of Maya to play with materialistic things, people and events. So long as we are satisfied with the cyclic pain and pleasures of this world and satisfied to wander in various species of living beings(84 lakh species), the God does not take us to his abode; but the moment we realise the flickering nature of the material world and realise its impermanent nature, when we get tired of the continuous pains and pleasures, the treachery of the relations, the bodily changes leading to diseased body, incapacitated body or towards death, and then we turn towards something beyond this material objects which we believe is controlling everything and is beyond that which we cannot comprehend with our materialistic vision i.e. Lord. So when we truly turn towards the Lord, the lord turns towards us. Then comes a particular method by which we can attain the divine love as mentioned in scriptures i.e. of loving remembrance of his name and form in addition to full surrender to the lord.

The lord himself gives instances of surrender of fruits of actions in Gita and loving remembrance of him to attain him in following verses.

Bhagavad Gita, Chapter 18, Sloka 11

न हि देहभृता शक्यं त्यक्तुं कर्माण्यशेषतः |
यस्तु कर्मफलत्यागी स त्यागीत्यभिधीयते ||18.11||

na hi deha-bhṛitā śhakyaṁ tyaktuṁ karmāṇy aśheṣhataḥ
yas tu karma-phala-tyāgī sa tyāgīty abhidhīyate

Meaning : For the embodied being, it is impossible to give up activities entirely. But those who relinquish the fruits of their actions are said to be truly renounced.

अनन्याश्चिन्तयन्तो मां ये जनाः पर्युपासते ।
तेषां नित्याभियुक्तानां योगक्षेमं वहाम्यहम् ॥ 22॥

ananyāśh chintayanto māṁ ye janāḥ
paryupāsate
teṣhāṁ nityābhiyuktānāṁ yoga-kṣhemaṁ
vahāmyaham

BG 9.22: There are those who always think of Me and engage in exclusive devotion to Me. To them, whose minds are always absorbed in Me, I provide what they lack and preserve what they already possess.

कर्मण्येवाधिकारस्ते मा फलेषु कदाचन ।
मा कर्मफलहेतुर्भूर्मा ते सङ्गोऽस्त्वकर्मणि ॥ 47

<u>**BG 2.47**</u>: **You have a right to perform your prescribed duties, but you are not entitled to the fruits of your actions. Never consider yourself to be the cause of the results of your activities, nor be attached to inaction.**

So in both ways if we don't have the right to entitlement to the fruits of our actions then why expect fruits of our karmas and get bonded with Maya. So in either way it is desirable and wise decision that we surrender to the lord both ourselves and our karmas with no sense of doer ship of the karmas to relieve ourselves of the future bondages arising out of such expectations.

Bhagwad Gita chapter 18 verse 66

सर्वधर्मान्परित्यज्य मामेकं शरणं व्रज |
अहं त्वां सर्वपापेभ्यो मोक्षयिष्यामि मा शुच: || 66||

*sarva-dharmān parityajya mām ekaṁ śharaṇaṁ vraja
ahaṁ tvāṁ sarva-pāpebhyo mokṣhayiṣhyāmi mā śhuchaḥ*

<u>**BG 18.66**</u>: **Abandon all varieties of dharmas and simply surrender unto Me alone. I shall liberate you from all sinful reactions; do not fear.**

Even the lord declares himself that a soul needs to surrender to Lord Krishna by abandoning all varieties of dharmas and attain freedom from Maya.There is no fear to the soul then as after surrendering to the Lord, the Lord takes total care of the surrendered soul. He destroys his sins and makes him attain his eternal abode.

Chapter 9- Why we need to seek spiritual knowledge from Vedic Scriptures, and realised saints.

A verse of Bhaja Govindam says that if we don't seek for the self knowledge or spiritual knowledge as who am I, why have I come to this earth, what is the purpose of my birth, where will I go after death etc. then they are destroyed in material hankerings and desires and so they fall into hell; meaning to say they do not attain the ultimate i.e the liberation from birth and death and again due to continues and endless materialistic pursuits, after this human form is destroyed are cast into hell i.e to other forms of human species where they wander aimlessly and continue to suffer hellish condition without ability to think, comprehend and attain knowledge to free themselves and attain Lord Hari. *This continues for 84 lakh species and again when the Lord feels compassion after millions of kalpas or yugas is a soul born as human being and again due to lack of knowledge repeats the same thing.* So it is very important we seek the superior transcendental knowledge.

कामं क्रोधं लोभं मोहं
त्यक्त्वाऽऽत्मानं भावय कोऽहम् ।
आत्मज्ञानविहीना मूढा-
स्ते पच्यन्ते नरकनिगूढाः ॥ २६॥

kāmaṁ krodhaṁ lobhaṁ mohaṁ
tyaktvā'tmānaṁ bhāvaya ko'ham |
ātmajñāna vihīnā mūḍhāḥ
te pacyante narakanigūḍhāḥ || 26

Leaving off desire, anger, greed, and delusion, make self-inquiry; who am I? They are fools who are without Self-knowledge; as captives in hell, they are tortured.

Verse from Naradha Pancharatra

Text 53

viṣaye baddha-cittaṁ ca

sarvam indriya-sevanam

poṣaṇaṁ sva-kuṭumbānāṁ

svātmanaś ca nirantaram

By cultivating material knowledge, people remain engrossed in thoughts of sense enjoyment and busy maintaining their family members.

Text 54

prathamaṁ sāttvikaṁ jñānaṁ

dvitīyaṁ ca tad eva ca

nairguṇyaṁ ca tṛtīyaṁ ca

jñānaṁ ca sarvataḥ param

The first and second *rātras* consist of knowledge in the mode of goodness. The third *rātra* contains the topmost transcendental knowledge.

The knowledge found in the fourth *rātra* is in the mode of passion and so the devotees do not desire to hear about it. The knowledge described in the fifth *rātra* is in the mode of ignorance and so learned people are not the least bit interested in it.

So these all comes under the purview of material knowledge and they can only create desires in human minds and bind the soul to the material world. So we need to go for the transcendental knowledge, i.e the real knowledge related to methods of attaining the divine abode, how to realise the Lord and what best should we do in this present age of quarrel and hypocrisy to attain the lord where no other practices are possible as yagyan, japa, tapa, penances etc.

So a devotee to gain that highest knowledge has to read the ancient scriptures. Not all but the basic which comprises of all the important teachings related to methodologies of realising the God and attaining devotional service to the Lord as Bhagawad Gita, Srimad Bhagawadam, Sri Ramcharit Manas etc. and Bhaja Govindam of Adi Sankaracharya. One should also patiently hear the discourses as presented by rasik and self-realised saints of India because by hearing or sravana we gain in-depth and quick knowledge as compared to reading. So both reading and hearing are important means to seek that divine knowledge of methods to attain love for God and get oneself freed from Maya.

Then there are technologies driven methods which can be of immense help nowadays in busy schedule of everyone. For eg. in You tube and Google we get to hear the discourses of learned saints and rasiks of Vrindavan, Ujjain, Triveni, Prayagraj, Ayodhya etc. and also we get to buy some basic scriptures and also other scriptures from online medium.

As previously described, in this age of quarrel and hypocrisy we have no strength and time left to go through various practices as we were doing in the other three yugas as satya yuga, treat yuga, dwapara yuga due to lack of time, less physical ability and other innumerable problems pertaining to present time of imperfections. So we can at least go through the basic Scripture of Bhagawad Gita and Srimad Bhagawadam which consists of the essence of the important scriptures of Hindu religion and help us to seek the transcendental knowledge to attain God.

Chapter 10. Realise the worldly relations and material achievements are transitory.

To make us aware that we don't have anything or can achieve anything that will be everlasting are one of the purpose of scriptures. The scriptures explains in depth that why we should not long after or cling to the material enjoyments, events, designations or relationships. It is simple that either you or the other one you are related to will leave the world earlier and again you remain without the person of attachment. Second there can be no guarantee that a person who is related to you and to whom you believe to be your own, will not change his mind-set as per his attitude or necessity and leave you if his motive with you is not fulfilled. Because the scriptures says every relationship in this world is motivated by selfish desires. Once you are of no use to someone, that person will not think of you twice.

As a verse from Ram Charit Manas speaks, that everyone has one motive behind making affection towards someone and it is selfish desires.

उमा राम सम हत जग माहीं। गुरु पितु मातु बंधु प्रभु नाहीं॥
सुर नर मुनि सब कै यह रीती। स्वारथ लागि करहिं सब प्रीति॥1॥ -

राम चरित मानस

अर्थ - हे पार्वती! जगत् में श्री रामजी के समान हित करने वाला गुरु, पिता, माता, बंधु और स्वामी कोई नहीं है। देवता, मनुष्य और मुनि सबकी यह रीति है कि स्वार्थ के लिए ही सब प्रीति करते हैं॥1॥

There is no security in worldly achievements and worldly relations because we have no guarantee that we and all our relatives live for 100 years or say a long life. There may be accidents, unnatural death, death due to disease, murder or suicide etc. Life is unpredictable and has no guarantee that one will live for 100 years. So we must be prepared for the worst. Anything may happen and we or our relatives may die. So let's be prepared for the worst. Here the author says be prepared for the worst means, to make yourself ready that even though death may come anytime uninvited we have to make our self ready with our spiritual knowledge and practices so that even if we die our soul will go to its destination beyond the cycle of birth and death.

Even Sri Kripaluji one renowned saint of India who has already left for heavenly abode, has written in his poem by his divine experiences, Radha Govind Geet on the impermanency nature of life as follows-

आयु जल बुलबुला गोविंद राधे।
जाने कब फूट जाये सबको बता दे ॥

- *जगद्गुरु श्री कृपालु जी महाराज, राधा गोविन्द गीत (956)*

आयु [मानव देह] एक पानी के बुलबुले जैसा है, किसी को नहीं पता यह कब फूट [समाप्त] हो जाए ।

Then secondly how much wealth one may make in this lifetime it may be stolen or wasted in unnecessary expenditure or god forbids any emergency may force you to give up all your wealth. So there is no need to feel secured because of worldly achievements as wealth, friends, relatives, knowledge etc. Because as said in Bhaja Govindam, that

मा कुरु धनजनयौवनगर्वं
हरति निमेषात्कालः सर्वम् ।
मायामयमिदमखिलं हित्वा
ब्रह्मपदं त्वं प्रविश विदित्वा ॥ ११॥

mā kuru dhana jana yauvana garvaṁ
harati nimeṣātkālaḥ sarvam |
māyāmayamidamakhilaṁ hitvā
brahmapadaṁ tvaṁ praviśa viditvā || 11

Do not be proud of wealth, kindred, and youth; Time takes away all these in a moment. Leaving aside this entire (world) which is of the nature of an illusion, and knowing the state of Brahman, enter into it.

So realising the impermanent nature of material existence and human life, and realising the purpose of human birth we have one duty yes only one duty i.e. to seek transcendental knowledge, go through our Vedic scriptures and listen from a self-realised saint cum preacher, about the scripture's   teachings and without wasting any more time. walk seriously on the spiritual path and attain our desired objective of attaining the life beyond birth and death and never ending happiness.

Chapter 11: Lord Krishna is the Ultimate Reality, and realising him, we attain freedom from the cycle of birth and death.

अहमात्मा गुडाकेश सर्वभूताशयस्थित: |
अहमादिश्च मध्यं च भूतानामन्त एव च || 20||

aham ātmā guḍākeśha sarva-bhūtāśhaya-sthitaḥ
aham ādiśh cha madhyaṁ cha bhūtānām anta eva cha

BG 10.20: O Arjun, I am seated in the heart of all living entities. I am the beginning, middle, and end of all beings.

When we say, we need to achieve a status where we are not born again and that is the only goal of human birth, first we need to realise whom to worship and whom to adore. So in simple term or layman language, realise that Krishna is the supreme Lord and we need to achieve his lotus feet and that can be done after realising and understanding the fact that God is the supreme. Now there are many Hindu Scriptures where it is said Lord Krishna or Lord Rama (another form of the Lord) is the ultimate God to whom we need to surrender, love exclusively and worship him out of devotion to go beyond the repeated cycle of birth and death. But the most authentic source is Srimad Bhagwad Gita and Srimad Bhagawadam where it is said by the Lord himself that he is the supreme power, he is all pervading, he is in all living being, he is indestructible, he is beyond the material nature, he is the only source of unlimited bliss and to attain him is the only purpose of human birth.

I here put forward some of the important verses from Srimad Bhagawadam and Sri Bhagawad Gita establishing the facts that Lord Krishna is the God, the Supreme and he is to be worshiped and he has innumerable forms but the prime form is that of Lord Krishna.

In the above sloka 20 of chapter 10, the lord clearly describes that he is the all pervading, he is the beginning, middle and end of everything i.e he is the creator, maintainer and destroyer of this unlimited universe. He is established in every living beings heart so he is the supreme soul yet divided into unlimited souls.

यो मामजमनादिं च वेत्ति लोकमहेश्वरम् |
असम्मूढ: स मर्त्येषु सर्वपापै: प्रमुच्यते || 3||

yo māmajam anādiṁ cha vetti loka-maheśhvaram
asammūḍhaḥ sa martyeṣhu sarva-pāpaiḥ pramuchyate

BG 10.3: Those who know Me as unborn and beginning less, and as the Supreme Lord of the universe, they among mortals are free from illusion and released from all evils.

Here in the above verse no. 3 of chapter 10 of Srimad Bhagwad Gita, it is clearly spoken by the Lord, that those who know the truth about the Lord i.e he is not born as us, i.e he is begin less, he has no origin, and he is the Supreme Lord of the Universe are actually liberated from Maya or illusion and released from all evils, here all evils means from the cycle of continuous material existence, suffering and wandering among 84 lakh species sometimes as a demigods as eg Indra, Brahma etc. sometimes as human beings in earth and other planets, sometimes as lower forms as animals, plants, birds etc.

महर्षय: सप्त पूर्वे चत्वारो मनवस्तथा |
मद्भावा मानसा जाता येषां लोक इमा: प्रजा: || 6||

*maharshayah sapta pūrve chatvāro manavas tathā
mad-bhāvā mānasā jātā yeshāṁ loka imāḥ prajāḥ*

BG 10.6: **The seven great Sages, the four great Saints before them, and the fourteen Manus, are all born from My mind. From them, all the people in the world have descended.**

The lord also says in the above verse no. 6, chapter 10, that he is the source of everything. Everything, all species of life actually originated from the Lord. Here in the above slokas or verse, lord Krishna says the seven sages, the four saints before them, the fourteen Manus were all born from the mind of the Lord i.e he desired them to be created and just they were born. Then from the Manus, all people of the world descended. This is to explain that the Lord is the original source of creation.

The Śhrīmad Bhāgvatam states:

> *ete chāṁsha kalāḥ puṁsaḥ kṛishṇas tu bhagavān svayam* (1.3.28) v6

"All the forms of God are the expansions, or the expansions of the expansions of Shree Krishna, who is the primordial form of God."

And so, the secondary creator Brahma prays to Shree Krishna:

> *yasyaikanishvasita kālamathāvalambya*
> *jīvanti lomavilajā jagadaṇḍanāthāḥ*
> *vishṇurmahān saihayasya kalāvisheṣho*
> *govindamādi purushaṁ tamahaṁ bhajāmi*
> (Brahma Samhitā 5.48)[v7]

"Infinite universes—each having Shankar, Brahma, and Vishnu—manifest from the pores of Maha Vishnu's body when he breathes in, and again dissolve into him when he breathes out. I worship Shree Krishna of whom Maha Vishnu is an expansion."

Here in the above verse of Srimad Bhagawadam, it is stated that there are innumerable and infinite universes. Each universe has one Shankar, Brahma and Vishnu. Infinite universes are created from one Maha Vishnu's, one-thousandandth or one millionth part of a bodily hair pore. And Maha Vishnu is created from one thousandth or one millionth of a pore of Lord Krishna's one bodily hair.

The Infinite Universe :Lord Krishna is the Supreme Creator

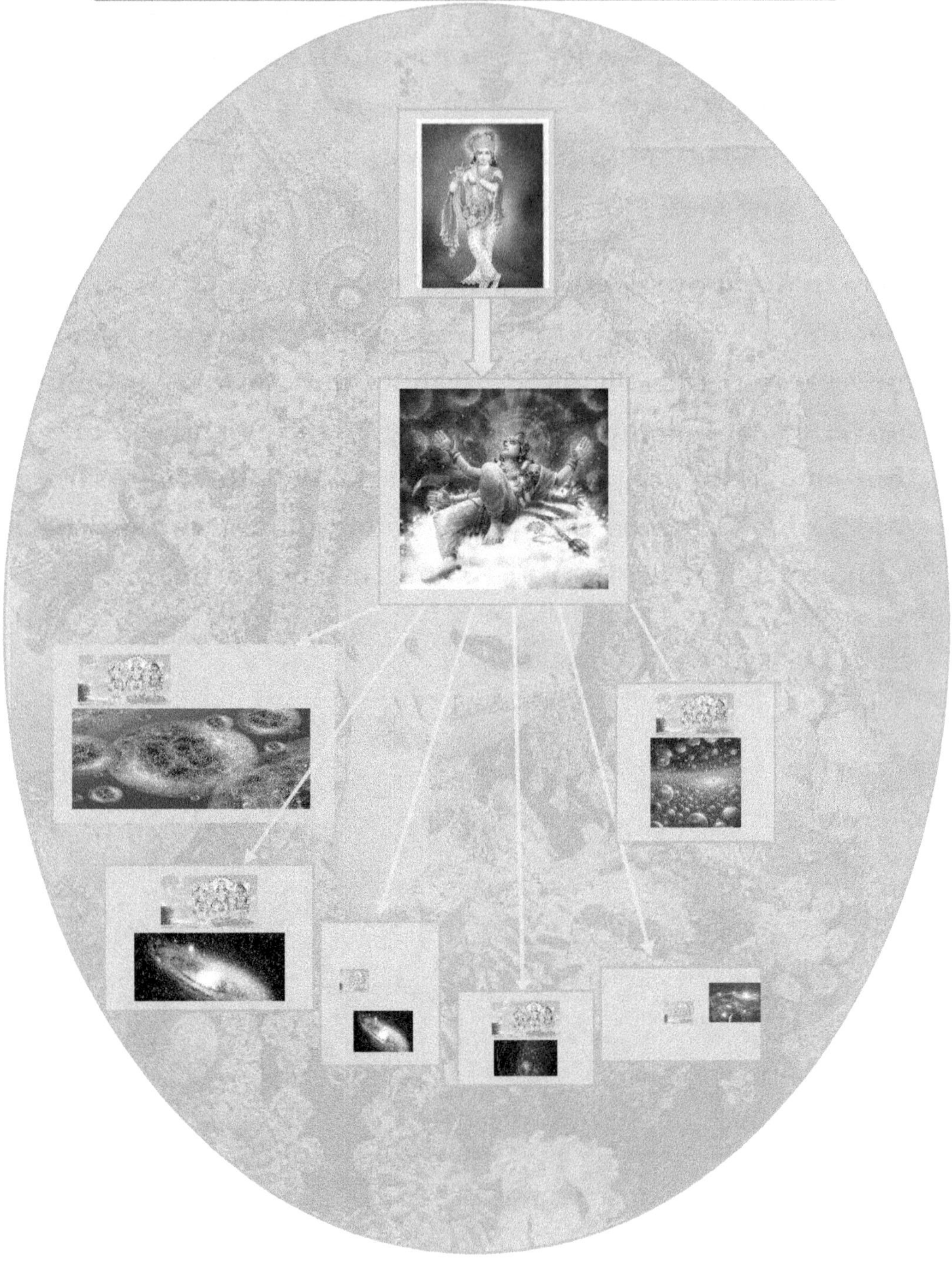

परं ब्रह्म परं धाम पवित्रं परमं भवान् ।
पुरुषं शाश्वतं दिव्यमादिदेवमजं विभुम् ॥ 12॥
आहुस्त्वामृषयः सर्वे देवर्षिर्नारदस्तथा ।
असितो देवलो व्यासः स्वयं चैव ब्रवीषि मे ॥ 13॥

BG 10.12-13: Arjun said: You are the Supreme Divine Personality, the Supreme Abode, the Supreme Purifier, the Eternal God, the Primal Being, the Unborn, and the Greatest. The great sages, like Narad, Asit, Deval, and Vyas, proclaimed this, and now You are declaring it to me Yourself.

In the above Shloka no. 12 and 13, of Chapter 10, of Srimad Bhagwad Gita, Arjuna the disciple, cousin brother and the friend of Sree Krishna speaks that Krishna is the Supreme Purifier, the Eternal God, the Primal Being, the Unborn and the Greatest. The great sages as Narad, Asit, Deval and Vyas had already said in various scriptures and in the Bhagwad Gita, the Lord himself declares the same that he is the Supreme Being. So from all the Vedic scriptures and Sastras it is proved that the Lord Krishna is the Supreme God and there should be no more doubt with relate to this fact. So realising this truth, any person can attain the highest truth and make oneself free from the pangs of sufferings of Maya and go beyond birth and death.

Skanda Purana Verse 14 and 15

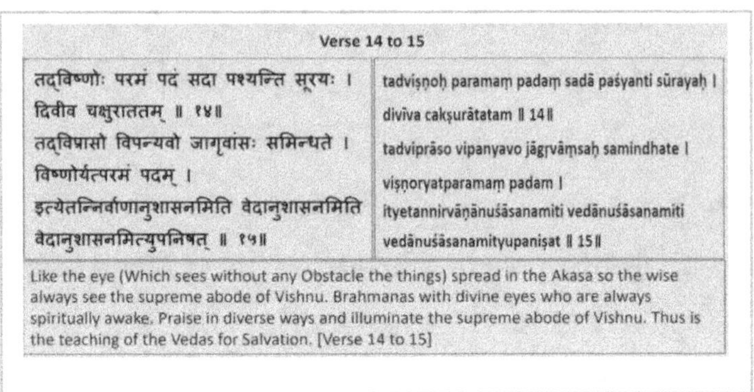

So in the above verse 14 and 15 of Skanda Purana; it is said that when one sees the supreme abode of Vishnu (Lord Krishna) with divine eyes who are always spiritually awake(fully conscious) and praise in diverse ways and illuminate the supreme abode of Vishnu, one attains liberation as per Vedas. So in other words, realising God, worshipping him with love (praising him) is enough to award us liberation.

Chapter 12: The Human Birth is like a water droplet on a lotus petal; it can fall at any time.

The human birth is transitory. All scriptures explains elaborately, life has no guarantee. We have no surety that we will live for seventy years, hundred years or any number as per our belief system. Death can come at any time and we have to be prepared for it.

Being prepared for death means, to complete our spiritual practices, self-realisation endeavours before the Lord of Death arrives. As the Yama or the Lord of Death do not ask our permission before taking us neither will allow us even a second from the destined time of our death to undo our mistakes of not doing the devotional practice to realise the ultimate truth, the Brahman.

In the Vivekachudamani written by Adi Sankaracharya, Shloka 3, it says as such-

> **These are three things which are rare indeed and are due to the grace of God – namely, a human birth, the longing for Liberation, and the protecting care of a perfected sage.**

So here also it is clearly mentioned that human birth is very important and is given to attain liberation. And after getting human birth if we get a perfected sage, who can give us knowledge of the Hindu Vedic Scriptures which will further help us in self-realisation, then what better than that. Again the desire to attain freedom from material existence i.e. liberation is also rare and is achieved by the Lord's grace.

Again in Vivekachudamani, Shloka 8, it is said as such-

> Therefore, the man of learning should strive his best for Liberation, having renounced his desire for pleasures from external objects, duly approaching a good and generous preceptor, and fixing his mind on the truth inculcated by him.

Katho Panishad-Part 2, Canto 3, Verse 4

इह चेदशकद्बोद्धुं प्राक्शरीरस्य विस्रसः ।
ततः सर्गेषु लोकेषु शरीरत्वाय कल्पते ॥ ४ ॥

iha cedaśakadboddhuṃ prākṣarīrasya visrasaḥ .
tataḥ sargeṣu lokeṣu śarīratvāya kalpate .. 4..

4 If a man is able to realise Brahman here, before the falling asunder of his body, then he is liberated; if not, he is embodied again in the created worlds.

So as per the above shloka or verse of Katho Panishad, it again explains that before death approaches, if a man realises Brahman here then he is liberated otherwise he is embodied again in the created worlds, so to say that he is again not born as human being but fall into various lokas as various forms of living entities.

So realising the nature of human birth, and its impermanent nature, we should seriously strive for spiritual realisation and quickly give up pursuits after material hankerings and go for self-realisation of the eternal truth, the Brahman.

Chapter 13: Chanting of the Lord's name is the simplest and only possible way of deliverance in this age of Quarrel and Hypocrisy (Kali Yuga).

कलयुग केवल नाम अधारा, सुमिरि सुमिरि नर उतरहिं पारा

In Ramcharit Manas, it is stated that in Kaliyuga i.e age of Quarrel and Hypocrisy, only name taking the name of the Lord will deliver us from the cycle of birth and death.

As stated in the Brahmanda Purana,

sahasra-namnam punyanam trir avrttya tu yat phalam

ekavrttya tu krishnasya namaikam tat prayacchati

The above verse explains that if one utters the name of Lord Shri-Krishna once, one obtains the same result that comes from chanting the entire visnu-sahasranama three times.

So taking the thousand names of Vishnu is same as chanting one name of Lord Rama, and three thousand names of Vishnu; that is to say, three names of Rama , equals one name of Krishna. Therefore, chanting once the name of Krishna gives the same result as chanting Lord Rama's name three times.

As per Hindu Scriptures, Shri-Krishna's name is certainly the supreme name. So we can take Lord Krishna name or any name of the Brahman as Rama, Hari etc. to attain liberation.

Another verse from Padma Purana says-

Nama cintamanih krishnas caitanya-rasa-vigrahah purnah
suddho nitya-mukto 'bhinnatvan nama-naminoh

In the book **Harinama Chintamani by Srila Saccidananda Bhaktivinoda Thakura**, the above verse from Padma Purana is explained as below.

{ The above sloka meaning is that the holy name of Krishna is transcendentally blissful. It bestows all spiritual benedictions, for it is Krishna Himself, the reservoir of all pleasure. Krishna's

harer nama harer nama harer namaiva kevalam
kalau nasty eva nasty eva nasty eva gatir anyatha

"In this age of quarrel and hypocrisy the only means of deliverance is the chanting of the holy name of the Lord. There is no other way. There is no other way. There is no other way."

(Bṛhan-Nāradīya Purāṇa)

So chanting the names of the Lord is the simplest and quickest method to attain the Lord because of the innumerable lacunas of Kali Yuga.

Kali Yuga is the worst among the four yugas because of its various lacunas. As described in the *Bhagavata Purana*, the qualities of Kali-yuga are as follows:

> yada mayanritam tandra
> nidra himsa vishadanam
> shoka-mohau bhayam dainyam
> sa kalis tamasah smritah

The above verse translation is:

"When there is a predominance of cheating, lying, sloth, sleepiness, violence, depression, lamentation, bewilderment, fear and poverty, that age is Kali, the age of the mode of ignorance."

Further the scriptures elaborately describe the symptoms of kali yuga with the following verses examples:

Why these qualities develop is further explained:

> prayena martya bhagavantam acyutam
> yakshyanti pashanda-vibhinna-cetasah

In the Kali-yuga the human beings will not offer sacrifice to God because their intelligence will be diverted by atheism."

> dharmam vakshyanty adharma-jna
> adhiruhyottamasanam

"Those who know nothing about religion will mount a high seat and presume to speak on religious principles."

vedah pashanda-dushitah

"The Vedas will be contaminated by the speculative interpretations of atheists."

Yet, besides these faults of Kali Yuga, the scriptures declare there to be one great quality of Kali-yuga:

kaler dosha-nidhe rajann
asti hy eko maha gunah
kirtanad eva krishnasya
mukta-sangah param vrajet

"Although Kali-yuga is an ocean of faults, there is still one good quality about this age: simply by chanting the names of Krishna, one can become free from material bondage and be promoted to the transcendental kingdom."

So because of these qualities it becomes difficult to attain the Lord or liberation by other elaborate practices as sacrifices, meditation, worship etc. which were being practiced in other yugas or time by the people to attain freedom from the repeated cycle of birth and death. So chanting the name of the lord is prescribed in the scriptures as only method recommended for this age of quarrel and hypocrisy. The lord is not different from his name. so when we chant the name of the Lord, the lord himself dances in the tongue of the person chanting the names. So this shows as   the Lord is divine so is his name. As the Lord consists of innumerable power, beauty, qualities so does his name. So we get benefitted by taking the Lord's name by getting delivered from this material existence and going beyond this ocean of birth and death to that eternal abode of the Lord where there is no pain, sufferings, only every increasing bliss (Ananda).